*A man needs to love and to hate at the same moment,*
*to laugh and cry with the same eyes,*
*with the same hands to throw stones and to gather them,*
*to make love in war and war in love.*
*And to hate and forgive and remember and forget,*
*to arrange and confuse, to eat and to digest*
*what history takes years and years to do.*

~ Yehuda Amichai

# Forgetting
## the Holocaust

*poems by Ron Charach*

Frontenac House
Calgary, Alberta

Book and cover design: Epix Design
Cover Image: "Israel: Beach-Caesarea", by Arnie Saxe
Author photo: Dan Roitner

**Library and Archives Canada Cataloguing in Publication**

**Charach, Ron**
**Forgetting the Holocaust / Ron Charach.**

**Poems.**
**ISBN 978-1-897181-46-1**

**1. Jews--Canada--Poetry.  2. Holocaust, Jewish**
**(1939-1945)--Poetry.**

**I. Title.**

**PS8555.H39834F67 2010    C811'.54    C2010-906699-5**

We acknowledge the support of the Canada Council for the Arts for our
publishing program. We also acknowledge the support of The Alberta
Foundation for the Arts.

 Canada Council
for the Arts    Conseil des Arts
du Canada

Printed and bound in Canada
Published by Frontenac House Ltd.
1138 Frontenac Avenue S.W.
Calgary, Alberta, T2T 1B6, Canada
Tel: 403-245-2491 Fax: 403-245-2380
editor@frontenachouse.com   www.frontenachouse.com

# TABLE OF CONTENTS

## Holy Land

# Diaspora

# How to Forget the Holocaust

In the words of Mr. Bandler,
janitor of our parochial school,
as our learned, portly principal,
Rabbi Théodore Gorlick, strode by,
half-crescent glasses on a cord,
"It's eezy to forget Da Holocaust
if you're a *Yeuro-peean intee-lektual*
who's never been *beat up!*"

And Gorlick, raised in Paris after the War,
master of the art of showing no sign of having heard,
ignored his proletarian critic, now paused in mid-sentence
to let the "Da Learn'd Rabbit" pass.

Bandler smacked a bristling fist
into his bear-trap of a hand
and whispered invectives
into the ear of his beloved German shepherd, Blackie,
who sniffed the schoolyard for
anti-Semites and self-contented Jews.

What could I know of Mr. Bandler's *Lager*,
his run-ins with the horrors
recounted by poets—Levi, Améry, or Celan
—learned suicides all!—and other Jewish writers who struggled
their names into anagrams of their old identities
to fit among a people who *don't*
have pogroms and The Shoah behind them.

> *This night brings a vision of Mother,*
> *alevah hashalom, truncated by depression,*
> *half alive/half dead—horrified*
> *at her slipping grip on life,*
> *with a 'doctor-for-a-son'*
> *unable to save her.*

*As she vanishes, I consider*
*my thinning thighs.*
*Forty years from Rabbi Gorlick and Blackie,*
*I've become a stick person,*
*the kind of "bahn-deet intee-lektual"*
*that Bandler despised,*
*my muscles, like my arguments,*
*caught in a fatal dissolve.*

From other *Lagers* there emerged many witnesses
more damaged than Mr. Bandler,
who quietly swore that reality
would never again be the same.

We were kids. Mr. Bandler's
unbridled rage echoed our own
at the life-sucking boredom
of eight-thirty-to-five-o'clock Hebrew School.
How we loved it when he mocked:
"*Rabbi Gorlick … Rabbi Gorlick … Rabbi Gorlick!* …
You know *vat iz da troble wit* Rabbi Gorlick?
Never been *beat up!*"

But what did Mr. Bandler gain by being *beat up?*
He, who eluded Nazi fire and left behind
"da vine-tasting Yeuro-peean *bon vivants*",
the ones who ignored the arbitrary arrests
and vast disappearances, an entire continent
who disregarded the long nightmare
of The Others, *Les Autres,*
*Les Juifs,*
and kept on savouring the aroma
of pungent cheeses and butter-crusted bread
that smelled so much sweeter than the foot
of a sleepless, hidden child.

This is what he gained: he could tell you which of all
the possible sad ends of any story
would be the one to come true:
*"Viet Nam, Viet Nam, Viet Nam …"*
Mr. Bandler growled, rising above the local
and the personal history,
*"You know how Yoonited States vill come back from Viet Nam?*

*Vithout da pants! Vithout da pants!"*

# Istanbul

Joe Bendit was an ancient Turkish Jew who made Canada home.
He smoked cigars thicker than his own thumbs
as he kept my parents up all night
with tales of perils unmentionable, as his wife, Rosie,
nodded dreamily while her man held forth,
she, who condensed the simple greeting, "How are you?"
to *"Ha-yoo?"* which was even simpler.

Joe's eyes engorged as he regaled my folks with what it is to tiptoe
over the steaming grates of Istanbul
whose screws might be loosened by thieves
so that heavy-treading tourists would fall through
only to be robbed or stripped
and sodomized. Or worse.

In the next room, my older brother slept
as I tried, in vain, to push off,
but Joe wouldn't lower his voice for anyone, or give
heed to my angry thumps on the windowsill,
*Talk quieter! Please ... Shut up!*

And long after Mr. Bendit finally took his leave,
drowsy wife Rosie in tow,
Dad, who never debated anything with his good friend Joe,
would hum, or sing very softly, for days,
*"Istanbul was Con-stan-ti-nople,*
*Now it's Istanbul, not Con-stan-ti-nople ..."*

# For the Polish Poets

*To Adam Zagajewski*

Forgive my spotting a "jew" in your name,
*Pan* Zagajewski, it was as
conspicuous as the eyes of the Jewish child
you turned into Persephone in your poem,
Persephone who went underground again
to the silent indifference of
a spectral bird—went underground and would,
some day, return.

Milosz, Szymborska, Zbigniew Herbert,
each of you condemned Poland's S.S. dance
with Hitler.
Some of you went Underground,
others were children of those who resisted
the night that ended at the border of the Polish woods
where so few found refuge.

What did you think about Art Spiegelman's graphic novel *Maus*
portraying your countrymen as pigs,
the Germans as cats, mice as the Jews?
Is it true, state officials assigned last names
like "Robak", meaning "worm", to immigrant Jews
so that they resorted to gentler acronyms
cobbled from the original Hebrew to name themselves anew?
My own, Charach, may stand for "*Chossin Rebbe Chayim*",
"the son-in-law of Rabbi Chayim",
proof, at least, that an ancestor married well.

Is it true that the Polish nobles who conquered the Ukraine
handed the keys to the Church of the Orthodox priests
to Jewish storekeepers for safekeeping,
fanning the flames that flared into
the pogroms of the Cossack rebellion?
I was fed this in grade five,
in the book *Kiddush Hashem,*
and I want to know more than I know.
There must be more to say from your point of view.
If history isn't over until its effects are gone,
God knows this story isn't done.

Now, on a visit to Yad Vashem in Jerusalem
I gaze up at the Memorial to the Deportees,
a cattle-car suspended, mid-air, on a truncated suspension bridge
a drop to nowhere—
Who can spot Persephone cowering
in a sunless corner where the frantic
clamber to relieve themselves
or press their mouths to the slats for air?

I have never been to Poland,
never went, as a teen, on The March of the Living,
nor shook hands with Lech Walesa,
the nimble-fingered electrician who loosened the wires
between Soviet and Polish states while still
managing not to cut off anyone's power.

A neat trick by an admirable man.
But forgive me if I pull up short
reading the last lines of "Dedication" by Milosz:

*They used to pour millet on graves or poppy seeds*
*To feed the dead who would come disguised as birds.*
*I put this book here for you, who once lived*
*So that you should visit us no more.*

I would like to stop visiting this topic,
to drink deep the collected wisdom of Milosz and Herbert,
call them my brothers, *achai,*
in the full aching Hebrew of the word.

It is said that the Romans flayed alive Rabbi Akiva,
until he finally understood the full meaning
of *The Shema,* the holiest prayer—

I almost wrote, "*our* holiest prayer"
but the word would not be written by me,
for I have not yet got
the Rabbi's forgiveness in my mouth,
to cry out, even in dying, "We are all one."

# Ludochka

Not for you the pleated skirts, you
who dazzled us in the coat closet
at the back of the class, butt slinking out
of the elastic-waisted jeans
you called "suicides".
Not for you the comfort of only being imagined,
as you slowly peeled yourself before
the rapt attention of our blessed eyes.

Just minutes ago our minds were a haze
of the strangest form of boredom, and awash
with those black-and-white films of
naked bodies in heaps at Birkenau
that Mrs Lesnitsky forced into our gaze.

Decades later, you and I would meet again.
Under pancake make-up
you played the vamp so well
no one would have pegged you
as offspring of a single mother with broken English,
you, who flashed your tomboy body for the boys
in a dark room of damp winter coats,
dripping scarves and limp mittens.

It took you a while to remember me.
But once, when you slowed the spinning
of your pelvis, you cast me a longing look
not as if you wanted me to want you more
than anyone else in that little room did,
but as if, in a way I only understood years later,
I might become an ally in your counter-
offensive to take back the flesh.

# The Choirmaster

Yours was a twin genius, the public one for musical
    arrangements,
the private, for shaming, coining *nicknames*
for every reticent soul in your choir.
You never missed
this one's body odour: *getootreh Shtink!*
that one's darker skin: *Schvartzer! Crow!*
a bad complexion: *pizza punim!*
two bits of pectoral fat on a shy boy: *titsum! Du, Titsum!*
or find flaws they could only imagine
in their cracking treble voices.

In tune with your agonized smile
and a surprise French kiss for a girl
invited on your knee,
you channeled all the red-loined energy
at your command and struck out
with your yardstick in the middle of a song—*Whack!*
for we sang poorly, always on the watch for your moods,
so poorly compared to the way you
once sang.

Only your survival in Nazi hands could explain you.
And when you died, our parents wept—wept!
The Jewish papers beamed
about your sacred arrangements,
your timing and your tempo.

It explained you, and how self-loathing could become
the measure of musical beauty; the right song
can still make even the strongest of us tremble
as you were still before him with your terrible baton.

Choirmaster, rise up. Take a bow,
you taught us well our worth in your purified
contempt all the years we were sent to you
by our parents' most desperate dreams.

# Synagogue

Feeling an imposter
in a burgundy robe more stately
than anything I will ever wear again, I take my seat,
two years shy of Bar Mitzvah,
not yet eleven.

Ah, but I found refuge in the mournful beauty
of the *Ayts Chayim* song,
one of the few I knew in English:
"It is a Tree of Life",
a lament, Mother, that years after your death
still summons your chestnut-haired beauty
like a dream remembered as silent—

The wealth of song makes me forget
the very first synagogue I sat in, the little Ashkenazer,
"The Ashcan", a run-down pillbox across the street
from stoney Anglican St. Giles,
(was it really a "Cathedral"?
How I tried to look away
from those superior spires.)

Yes, the Ashcan was a synagogue, if less ritzy
than this later one into which I bought my way
with a still-evolving voice.

But even the Ashcan was pricey for Father
who was too strapped, too cautious, or too cheap
to buy a Yom Kippur seat.
And the only house of worship I was ever asked to *leave*.

The man who shook me down
for lack of a ticket
wore a gold ring, a raw silk tie
and a "Sorry, but—" look,
for my failure to be a complete Jew,
an officially seated Jew.

And on *Simchat Torah,*
the celebration of receiving The Law,
when the adults were dancing down the aisles,
Mr. Kane the candy manufacturer
handed chocolates to his grandchildren
and who-knows-who-else's kids,
but when my turn came, he said,
"Sorry, Sonny, I would give you some,
but my hands are so warm
the chocolate would melt ..."
How I regretted my blonde hair and green eyes,
though Mom thanked God every day
that I didn't look Jewish.

In the night scene in *Taras Bulba:*
the Polish cavalry waving torches
stampedes down the streets:
*"There's a Cossack in the city!*
*There's a Cossack in the city!"*
*(Hide your women! Hide your gold!)*

No banishment from ceremonial wine
can make me the Cossack or the Pole I look,
or make Baba forgive the comparison
with either.

Yet my Burrows Avenue eyes would plunder
those glittering Torah crowns
with their huge costume jewels,
as I strained to see inside the teak doors
before they slid shut:
The Ark of the Covenant,
an atmospherics of gilded lions,
sheet lightning, and wondrous wrath
in the desert.

I swore then I would make it
far enough into life
to give thanks to God, and mean it.
One day I would look around the synagogue I sat in
without having to guess at each family's wealth,
the sheer cost of its evidence.

# Jewish Grain

*For Rabbi Bernard Baskin*

Our senior rabbi tells
of how his father, *The Rahv*,
an orator schooled in three sacred tongues,
would enter his synagogue in New York
for a Friday night service,
and cause, as he strode the red carpet,
row after row of men to rise from their seats
out of respect for his great learning.

*"It was like the undulations*
*in a field of wind-swept wheat,*
*these souls swept by faith*
*who could still believe in Man*
*as well as God."*

# Passover

On *Pesach*, it is said,
the home becomes a synagogue,
but not until after the endless tidying,
cooking, and negotiating are complete, not until the hosts
decide where to seat the sisters whose families don't get along
or the brothers-in-law who had the falling out,
or the young cousin awkward in groups of more than two—
then wondering for a terrified moment
whom this year they forgot to include.

In the *Seders* of my youth,
famished elders made a virtue of mumbling
the Passover story in thick *Ashkenaz,*
short-shrifting the *Haggadah* Hebrew,
eager to arrive at the festive meal.
They seldom paused, as we now do,
to illuminate the symbols
adorning the sacred plate.

Thank God for the Four Questions.
Even the family leader fell hushed
like everyone at the double long table,
as the youngest, for once, escaped being *shushed,*
and stood on a chair for a first performance
he had worded by heart.

Ah, the scent, the spirit,
the *ruach* of the occasion:
pungent red horseradish *chrayn*
suffusing apple/walnut *haroseth,*
a mock mortar sealing
two walls of brittle *matzoth*
as parched lips served as sounding bells
for the minor chords and gutterals
of the Hebrews' ancient tongues.
What magical effects,

hunting the *Afikomen* matzoh
as Manischewitz or Carmel red wine
tingled a still-developing brain
—any child could feel the prophet Elijah
brush by to the proffered cup of wine,
the sign that bedtime was long overdue.

To the unsympathetic,
our yearly recitation of the ten plagues
is the oldest grudge in the world.
Not so at the *Seder* of my adult years where
every portion on our collective plate
has a name someone alive remembers in family blood:
the Holocaust, the Russian exodus,
the release of the Falashas from the kingdom
of Ethiopia, the freeing of American slaves,
each hearkens back to the ancient revolt
that forged a nation out of servitude,
as Moses led his dispossessed
through forty years of desert,
torn between a golden calf
and a God only visible in achingly
brief pillars of smoke and fire,
but who gave of himself to his people
in a rain of heavenly manna
and a parted sea of grief.

*At this Seder may our story compete*
*with the daily demands of life.*
*Let food vie with song*
*for pride of place in the spirit.*
*May the last of our blood to be spilled*
*be an overturned glass of concord red*
*on a tablecloth of finest linen*
*stirring a frantic search for a mound of salt*
*in the middle of this, our people's freedom*
*and its great golden age.*

For all that, for all that, I, the father, find my seat
at the table's side, and I invite my cousin's wife,
a fine teacher, to lead our family *Seder*, "Order,"
I joke, "never having been my thing."
But all those rabbis' elderly eyes looking on—
and I ask myself, how can I stand there holy?

Prairie Water

# Hecla Island, Lake Winnipeg

What travelers will remember
is the road,
the would-be ancient causeway
that reformed the islanders
of their isolated ways.
Unreal as privacy,
built in '71,
it rolled the world in all year round,
though the portion that is paved
like a high-tech pier through the town
is less than a half-mile long.
Visitors scratch up their wagons and vans
just getting there, a vague initiation
to what is never fully entered.

Sixty families
forced to move back to the mainland
in the very early '70s; now
the five remaining brightly pastel buildings
are meant to make you think
of Iceland.

"Somehow it isn't
what I'd *expected,*"
you said
as you panned it,
propped on an elbow in bed.
Disappointment
in Lake Winnipeg's largest island
"that boasts a rugged shoreline,
rich in moose and a vast array
of waterfall,"
pelicans and heron
where they just couldn't be.
I began to worry you were right,
that from the vast human Overlook
it's always too early or too late
to spot the deer.

Remember that vacation
when we put so much repellent on
that no one approached us?
That's the way we want it,
tight control
over who puts the bite on us
for blood and company.
Long after you fell asleep
I sat up in the cottage living-room
of darkly stained paneling
and second-rate furniture;
every few minutes a new kind of bug
would wander in.
Now a dusty miller
richocheting in the tunnel of light,
now an insect so small
it could only be guessed at
by its flying lanes.
Always the spiders in waiting
who see in every housefly
a dark, beefy round,
finding the mosquitoes quite bony
but for the squirt of warm blood in them.

How many were dispatched by two-way radio
from the "managed marsh",
their homes paved over
when the highway came in?

I have never been moved by those Morisseaus
that show the mosquito as a god
six times the size of a canoe,
though an endless supply of them
would drain in courage
what it left behind in the heart.
I remain a "single mosquito man",
one mosquito per sensitive type,
and the moment one comes into view,
I understand:

*This* is what my two-year-old means
when he pulls at his ear:
something very strange
has been happening—*here,*
some high-pitched whine
there will never be a word for.

Just one of these can burst through
the membrane of my dreaming.
Impossible to spot on busy sheets
and no point trying to kill
on a shag rug;
But it's four a.m., too dark to search
these rosy-brown walls.
Mercy on my half-acre forehead,
you micro-thing,
hovering siphon, weightless
yet so able to take off anyway.
But here comes the little bastard
to bite me *again!* Circling—
my personal mosquito, liking my taste
but unimpressed
with my defenses,
a random swatting and waving about
of tormented King Kong arms.
Still less with the cartoon of me
fumbling for a flashlight,
or the dresser lamp
—attract in more if I have to—
but the only way sleep will ever come
is if I finish off
*this* one.

In the domestic dark of the cabin,
the wife sleeping ruthlessly well,
faint rustlings come
from my son's room
and jar me from reading
about forces that torture
but are only obeying orders—
All I dare do
is stand
and head for the blackened hall,
stomach muscles tightening
into a small round mirror.
Entering the bathroom
—a little bit closer—
I pull it out, reckoning
What manner of beast will interrupt
a mildly pissing man?

And watch a daddy-long-legs climbing slowly
through the unpredictable
groaning.
*Go to bed;*
*never mind what's in the next room.*
*What if the boy has sprouted talons?*
*or rushes out to greet me*
*with much older eyes?*
*Let the dawn arrive*
*and such things dissolve*
*on their own.*

Next morning
the cottage reclaimed from the ether,
my wife tells me our son
somehow wriggled out of bed
and spent half the night
under a wooden chair.
"What if he'd woken up
and hit his head!"

How to tell her
that faint rasping breath
on a night out at Hecla
—from a creature
who shares my toothbrush—
had me riveted.
Tell her of islands I head out to
when she falls asleep and leaves me
to my cycles,
escapes to a land
where night-fearing souls
turn into minds
that buzz like bulbs,
minds so knowing
no devil would come
within a book of them.

Overcast at the swimming-hole
I wade into the chilling waters,
looking too much myself
as I negotiate the sharp rocks,
and think of all the men and women
who retire from life
to articulate their pain.
Treading towards the orange buoy
far out and ablur,
I shrug off the urge to fail,
to sink,
and start committing
the awkward stroke

that always takes me further
than it has the right to.
Mid-way my temples sound
the alarm,
*This water isn't getting any warmer.*

Still I head out,
a witness to catastrophe
who is no longer needed,
because there are so many others,
trying to settle a mind with
a body's activity.

Then catch glimpses
in the lake of shadows
—of a face—then another—
then a long thin arm,
a woman's? a man's?
Could it be Hopkins or Hardy
or Dickinson,
whipping white light
out of the cold grey waters?
To swim alongside them,
struggling—
even for a moment.

# The Dock Spider

## I.

I can't look away as
a clean-shaven tarantula of the North
scales our abandoned boat shoes,
ignoring like a king
our barefoot water-tubing party of ten.

*"Kill it, kill it!"* screams a girl who spots it,
as it leaves the shoes, and fingers
the length of the dock in broad daylight.

The local boat repairman claims,
"One of these wouldn't leave my boat,
so I swung my hammer and took off her legs.
She was a big fat mama with an *egg-sack*—"
italics his, emphasizing his disgust as if the
greatest crime of loathsome things is to want more life.

"There's a limit to how big you let 'em get," he says,
master of natural law, and with a swift jerk he swings
the outboard engine around to the spider's destruction,
squishing it to the dock into a pulpy mess of quivering legs.

## II.

*"Gross!"* a child cries, and I too shiver.
From a seasoned fisherman, "Why the hell you do *that*?
Do you know how many *mosquitoes and black flies*
this gal could have eaten?

"Besides, they're not cloned;
each one of 'em's unique."

I'm thinking of my serious, tasselled ancestors who
wore only black and invited the stigma of being Other
because Other was the self that they had,
no matter what anyone else would do about it,

but I blurt out the joke instead:
"If one this size ever got into my cottage,
I'd put it up for sale."
"Which, the cottage, or the spider?"
And everyone laughs.


III.

The humanitarian in our group reasons an answer,
and a warning: *"Anything that eats other insects can also bite."*
So even its diet is a threat. Where have I heard that before?
Still, I shake out my boat shoes when I claim them
before heading uphill from the dock.

But I make a promise: from this day,
I will trap spiders *live*
and neither squash them in basements

nor vanquish them under sole.
I will not be like those men
who motorboat and canoe
but are afraid to swim.

With this oath, I head for the lake
and my hands tingle
with unfamiliar blood.

# Breakaway

The Cliftons leant me a rusty stake
to dislodge a breakaway piece of bog from my shore,
but it's a toothpick against this stinking tonnage.
Aware of my age and city-slicker status,
Mrs. Clifton, who winters here, offers,
"Call Frank. *He'll* know how to move it along."

Frank arrives in a pick-up.
Paunchy, balding,
five years my junior,
but he's weathered as a petroglyph,
and has a helper, a beanpole teenager
already ruddy in the face.

"Ya got t'git the water *underneath*
and let her do the liftin',
like one of them glaciers
that carved out one of them canyons
—not much speed, but plenty o' power."

That's their technique,
and in ten minutes the little island

is heading back into the lake
towards someone else's frontage.

"What do I owe ya?"
"Twenty.
Put your docks in fer fifteen more."

"So, you're as good at lodging things
as getting them to move?"

"Pardon?"

"Okay, you guys do the docks.
I got a big patch of field to mow."

He eyeballs it.
"Fifty, and that's done too.
Buddy here rides a mean mower.
Don't ya, Buddy?"
*Let's see: Fifty dollars*
*+ a twelve-pack of appreciation*
*= peace of mind.*
*More time to write, to swim …*

*City mouse, country mouse,*
*city louse, country grouse.*

"It's a deal."

Before they start on the lawn,
Frank takes me aside:
"Mrs. Clifton says you're a doctor.
You know anything about
that whole *stagin'* business,
you know, Stage I, Stage II …?"

"A bit …"

"The wife has a Stage III
and it don't look good."

"What's the er, primary, um,
where did it start?"
"Bowel, large bowel,
but some of it must've broke off,
'cause now it's in
her bones."

"Oh. I'm so sorry.
How is she handling it?"

He narrows his eyes,
"What kind o' medicine you do?"

"Psychiatry—"

He removes his baseball cap,
wipes the sweat from his brow,
pushes back a crest of graying hair,
winks at Buddy.
"*That*'ll pay the bills …"

# On a Winter Walk

with my twelve-year-old Labrador
around the ice-encrusted bowl of ravine,
a million mounds and craters sparkling in the moonlight,
I breathe through a wraparound scarf
and conjure desert places with powdery sand,
perhaps Mozambique,
as in a photo I have of a young tree
forcing its way up through a gravestone.

Looking up at a dark city sky poor of stars
I think of Eliot's "The Wasteland"
and "Fire and Ice" by Frost,
as searching for the dog, disappeared
behind a blank ridge,
I feel the losses to come, in order,
of my family physician,
the accountant who can read my writing,
my brother, close friends,
my wife, my daughter, my son—

On a solitary walk, slight breeze from the north
and the crunch of snow too lively to be real,
glasses fogging, ears numbing with December,
I step flatly on the ice; it's the pace of middle age
trying to skirt an expanse
that marries the inevitable
with the unforeseen.

My brain starts to beat time,
updates the old Holocaust litany:
*Grozny—Beslan.*
*Sabra and Shatilla—Natanya!*
*Lower Manhattan—Fallujah!*
*Rwanda—Darfur.*

My God, *where's that dog!*

But *there* he is, *there*—
broad nose speckled with snow as he fumbles at a stick
that used to be easy.
*How will we ever find our way home?*

# Devotional

Brent went on a devotional solo
at the edge of the woods,
(church organizers never thought about mosquitoes)
the tea candles so filled to the brim with their bodies
that they actually exploded.

Only one of his friends made it through,
having decided to assume "a dignified posture"
and thereby pass a nearly sleepless night,
only to awaken the next morning
with deformed arms and the swollen face
of true devotion.

Working Life

# Minimalist

A modern classical
composer friend wonders
if his craft was shaped

by his first job
as grounds keeper
in a sprawling graveyard.

Each day of cutting and raking
ended with a ride
in a pick-up, pulling up

to a mountain of flowers
choked by plastic
into early decay.

To mask the stench
he smoked and watched
dozens of earwigs scurry

through the ruined chorus
like metallic off-notes.
He blew smoke on the bugs,

guilty as one tormenting
a pet, or turning up the volume
to drown out parents fighting downstairs.

It wasn't easy at the end
of his shift to linger
mid the slabs of marble

and read out all the familiar
names. Or note the background
music growing more random
as he returned
to a once-loving home.

# S.O.A.P.

To document the progress of patients
today's intern uses the format
Subjective, Objective, Assessment, Plan: S.O.A.P.
Case in point: a long-haired, bespectacled man
brought in at midnight to Emerg.

Subjective: "I'm the lowest of the low." (Long pause.)
    "That's it. That's all you need to know."
Objective: Pale, disheveled middle-aged Caucasian male lacking I.D.
    Expressionless. Paucity of movement, speech.
    No evidence of vis./audit. hallucinations.
Assessment: Major depression.
    Rule out head trauma, schizophrenia, dementia.
Plan: Re-assess when more able to communicate.
    Suicide watch. Vitals Q2H.
    Blood work to rule out organicity.
    Attempt to locate family.

The method organizes thought
—though at first I balked at making SOAP
from the boiling pot of human woes.
Profound depressions all look the same.

As I probe this man's good vein
he holds his arm out
like a branch that ends in his hand,
gazing ahead, as in a dream.

"Next week," I answer, "things will be different.
Your sadness is confusing you."
But his expression remains the same.
That's it. Nothing more,
though much more I need to know.

# Cancer of the Vulva

It was born of defective immunity
coupled with a bout of HPV gone wild.
The result was triple-threat surgery:
two external bags and *pelvic exoneration.*

The family grieved for their poet daughter,
pleading to save her clitoris, all privacy long gone,
but after surgery and radiation, there remained
the threat of fistulas, and worse.

In lieu of passion, pain killers flowed.
*Send no Mapplethorpe flowers ...*

At the change of dressings, she looked up
and told the nurse, as if seeking a less vulnerable sister,
"Who will even look at me now?"
On the departure of the night nurse, she takes up a pen.
Before she leaves the hospital, she gives me this poem:

*CA VULVA*

*These pouting lower lips, now stripped from their cords*
*Were gateways to encounters, desire its own reward.*
*Drop them in a post-op bucket, close what remains like a purse;*
*May the long road to sexless survival replace any lyrical verse.*
*No more will a throb in my body open the gates of my heart;*
*All the unrehearsed recitations will fall flat as sensation departs.*
*Pare away at this bestial cancer, pare away at the seat of my lust,*
*Whet your knife on your surgical training, and continue to do what*
*    you must.*
*But be still about 'positive outcomes'; make no effort to cheer me in vain,*
*Give me nothing but long, pregnant silence, and narcotics to cope*
*    with the pain.*
*For I will awake from my slumber remembering all that I miss,*
*The slow rise of desperate excitement, the fire-in-the-genitals kiss.*

# The Adjudicator of Pain

"Forget what you know about pain," says the specialist
from the mansion across the false creek,
"think nociceptive verses neuropathic
and you're never far away from the truth."

He assesses for insurance companies;
it's lucrative work paying three times the government-funded rate.
He boasts a two-million-dollar fund
he can access for the most desperate cases,

but he lets slip that it's the *minor* accidents
with the greatest *apparent* disability
that he has no patience with,
the "chronic-fatigue/fibromyalgia types."

"They're intent on defeating
any helpful suggestion;
they embrace their pain
rather than fight it, you know?"

I don't think I do.
How many just claims does he
unfairly dismiss
for those premium-collecting firms?

How many souls are left
outside the gates of mercy? Suffering
and wondering themselves how they ended up
where *every* sentence that begins with
*Forget what you know about pain*
ends up—*far away from the truth.*

# No One Shakes Hands Any More
*April 2003, Toronto*

I.

She's a regular at this stop,
midriff exposed in the current fashion,
slim, blonde, pretty, in a way now common
with multiply-pierced ears and a diamond-studded nose.
She has two children, an older boy
who avoids her watchful gaze,
and a younger, in closer tow.
She warns them with her eyes:
*don't touch that hand rail; step back*
*from that Chinese guy with a cough!*
Both kids are frowning.
Her brow is tense with a truth
every laureate should know:
no occupation as demanding
as that of a mom alone in the city with two kids

—save, perhaps, that of another regular,
the Philippina nurse at the far end of the car
on her way to a S.A.R.S. ward
to labour under double masks
performing intubations, with death exhaling
at both ends of the device.

At eye level, an ad for Covenant House,
*Cut a cheque for a street kid,*
competes with *Improve your sex life.*
The boys ignore their mother, and each other,
and now, as in Hong Kong,
handshakes and kisses are on hold in Toronto.
Slowly the train pulls away from the stop
in air still free of mutant virus.
Is this all we can ask,
a begrudging respect for each other's ways,
the generosity of distance?

II.

*"Hey, bleeding heart!"*
A deliberate, high-pitched voice from the end of the subway car:
*"Hey, liberal whiner, tsitser,*

"You mourn 'the handshake and the kiss'
but the only generous thing
about your 'begrudging respect'
*is* its distance!
Outside the consulting room, you're all, *tsk, tsk,*
but you step around the beggars on your way home,
and close your eyes right before a collision
so you won't have to spend time
in a witness box.

"*Do* something for the victims of S.A.R.S.—
or did you 'give at the office'—or worse, are you 'giving'
in these sacred, printed words?
Go write something useful, like that cheque."

I spot him, a fellow poet, exiting the train
as the double doors slide open, and close behind him,
his performance complete.

# Paper Wasps

*A quiet Sunday in the recession of 2008-09*

"Okay, here's my situation," I tell Cain Pest Control
(if anyone knows how to deal with pests, it's a guy named Cain),

"I have two third-floor dormers,
a good 25 feet above the flat roof
at the back of the house.
Hornets are flying in and out of a hole
and now inside the dormer wall
there's little ticking noises
all day long."

"Twenty-five feet, eh?
We'll send a guy with ladders. Cost you $180.
Work is guaranteed."

"In an unmarked van?"

"We can do that."

He pulls up in a white truck,
a tall, gaunt figure, 50 or 55,
hard to tell.
I ask him his name. It's Greg,
but he looks like a Clint.

He shades his eyes with his hands
and gazes up into the glare.

"How long they been there?"
"A few days."
"Small nest, then."

He heads to his truck and returns with
a transparent, bulbous device
filled with poisonous white powder.
He wears no protective clothing,
nothing to cover his face.

He scales the wall onto the flat roof,
hauling the shorter ladder with him.
Approaches the second storey
to survey his quarry at close range.
"You need a mask?" I shout,
wondering if I should offer him an N-95
from my swine-flu-epidemic stash.

"Paper wasps," he says, ignoring my offer.
"Bugs are the easy part.
The pitch of your roof,
now, that's hard on the knees."

He gets intimate with the entrance hole,
wedges in his contraption and starts pumping;
the powder flecks the dark shingles
and small white plumes waft back at him.

When he's done, he edges down,
carrying the small ladder with him,
then returns for his poison gun.
He wipes it off with a bandana.

Tells me to write the cheque to an Italian name,
not his own, and not Cain Pest Control.
On an unmarked receipt he laboriously prints:
*Wasps. Waranty.*
I tip him a ten-spot, but he seems indifferent.
"I only do weekends. Work these days is hard to find."

Then he tells me, for $80 he can caulk in every hole
where bees, wasps, even squirrels and raccoons
might enter;
then offers to remove a baby tree
growing in the top of my chimney.
"That's a bigger job; $100-plus;
means going up a much longer ladder,
with a bucket of cement."

I look up at the looming chimney
where he proposes his risk
for what I would have called
my own small nest till now.
"You *insured* for a job like that?"
"Just disability—like anyone else.
Can't afford the other."

# Monarch: A Painting

Fallen monarch, purchased for $800
in a gallery for orphaned artists
who toil in juried competitions,
you were no prize: would I even own you

if not for the painter's story of your creation?
In Temagami old-growth forest,
she tells me, she found your dead body,
sprayed it with fixative,

and used it to stencil three impressions
on a thick swath of hand-made paper,
then mounted your orange-black husk
as the finishing touch in the centre.

Art in the wilderness: the skies opened up
and forced a hurried rescue under blankets,
the only damage a slight running
of the background paint.

Your resurrection theme
suited our renovation:
the shimmer of white homemade paper
toned down our dusky-rose walls.

Centered over a floral sofa, you filled the hole
vacated by *Emphasis Mine*, a dramatic piece
that hung there peacefully for years
despite its violent imagery of
a nun stabbing Katherine Hepburn in the back,
which we donated to the AGO for respite and a fat receipt.

But when we tried to hang you,
the heavy plywood backing
burst through your flimsy frame,
landed on my foot and fractured my instep,

as if to mock the easy flight,
if not of your glued body,
then of your three pale shadow-mates.

While I healed, you sat in the limbo
beside the living room bookshelves,
resting until we had you re-framed
at a pseudo-gallery filled with decorator art.

When the reno was done, there was no room for you.
We considered a lawn sale,
even abandoning you by the curb
to scavengers. But that was where you started, wasn't it?
Some stories should not come full circle—
at least not *that* literally.

We hung you on the second-floor landing
whose taupe walls gave your background a lambent glow,
or was it, as in the galleries,
a flattery of skylight and halogen?

Now when I limp the stairs to the landing
you astonish me, Monarch,
presiding over your imprint offspring,
you, who are proof to a man with a bum foot
of an afterlife found at the end of sympathy
for art no art snob would countenance
or condone.

# Sturdy Shawcross Gloves

The old man I take my gloves to,
lined with fleece for Winnipeg winters,
inspects them in the muddy autumn light
of his shop in downtown Toronto.

For six bucks, he'll make them like new.
He usually works with shoes.
The leather will be treated;
he promises I won't need a new pair
for years, and gone will be
all the cracks and lines of toil.

Outside, it's twenty-five below,
and he can't afford to lose heat
out the fume hood, so we inhale
the aerosols together while I wait,

and he forces his thick fingers
that deal with God-knows-what solvents,
into the fingers of my gloves.

After two sprayed coats, he uses
—*snub-nosed pliers!*—to remove
each now-shiny glove from its rack
and bids me hold them while they dry.

I pay and leave, my gloves like new,
and so stretched they could belong
to my older brother,
or my dearly-departed dad,
another sturdy yet tippy man
who never in his life missed
a railway-station day of work.
Back in my office, the gloves
are macabre, wizened hands,
without recognizable history or
imaginable intent, but exuding
the pungent air of class collision
from a coat rack.

Later that evening, I arrive
to an essay written by my daughter
and resting on the kitchen table.
Appended to it, she's left
a yellow post-it note:

*Dad, you can read this, but don't get it dirty,*
*and please don't make any changes!*

# Mylar

*After an exhibition by artist Betty Goodwin*

Betty, what images you keep adding,
layer by diaphanous layer,
to a backdrop of acrylic or gesso
that beams forth the blue browns,
deep grays and rich greens of the earth

even as photographer Cindy Sherman,
your artistic opposite,
snaps at the lineaments of the human form
and finds them sorely
in need of alteration.

See how Cindy stretches her own face,
much the way Diane Arbus
displayed the distorted faces of others,
how she uses costumes to traverse centuries
in an effort to center each era
in her particular body

even as you post afterthoughts
on the see-through evanescence
of unrolled Mylar. The surface
is never enough, is it? Even
for photographers.

Art works this way, and I can't help it.
In my own mind now, I see the
imaging machines and biopsies
that display the blighted pinks, humid browns,
and oxygen-rich reds beneath
our own curvaceous and fragile skins,
pictures at the exhibitions
I've been seeing all my life
of what, in the soft light of reflection,
we dared to call good health
and tried to live within.

# Tubemonsoon.com:
## "Sexy French Canadian Girl on Girl"

The video-maker explains to the only vaguely listening blonde,
"We put an ad in the paper. A girl called. She'll be here any second."
In she steps, brunette, but like the blonde, stylish in black,
expecting a photo session, yes, but nothing like this.
In stages, the man who calls the shots convinces her to play along.
"Stand next to her, caress her; she doesn't bite. Now, give her a
      slow, deep kiss."
He's nicer than most porn directors. He's Canadian.

The new girl also has long, wavy hair, but is more squat,
with a tell-tale missing tooth on the side of her smile.
She answers sweetly: "No, I never want to kiss a girl,
yes, I have  a boyfriend, I love him. I only like the guys."
She knows the long-haired blonde is her aesthetic superior,
and when invited to kiss her lips, then breasts, acquiesces,
gingerly asking permission, "Is okay with you?"

Her deference to the blonde every step of the way
achieves erotic empathy quite rare in porn,
She seems delighted by the stroking and tasting.
"Is good, *so* good!" she shares with the director (and the film),
and after allowing herself to be pleasured by the lovely, jaded blonde,
crows, "She is *good!* She has one too, so she *know* how to do it! …"

But I grow restless as the discoveries yield
to the usual strap-on gear,
and orgasms that seem hard like work,
just another gig
to repay a debt or make rent or maybe get
that dental implant.

Half an hour is a long time
to be nude under klieg lights,
your every grunt and sigh on tape,
trying to prevent gas or worse from getting out
(or me from thinking that).

If only this weren't just a brunette, whose breasts
are unequivocally real, and an altered blonde,
who's seen this many times before,
and for whom being kissed "down there"
is nothing to get excited about any more—

this naked lunch to please
300,000 hits' worth of audience
and an aging voyeur with a poem in his hand.
Nothing has changed and no one
was worse off for the encounter.
And the man with the camera?

In resolute control, he seemed,
(*his* hair was black, in a pony-tail),
but for a fleeting moment of uncertainty
he detected in the feigned pleasure of the blonde,
and the way a working-class brunette
seemed happy to cheat on her boyfriend, taking
something her life would never have given
if everything in it had gone the way it should.

# The Jewish Problem

Harold Bloom has read it all
and recast a portion of the Bible
as "The Book of J."

And how seductively posed was Harold Brodkey,
who, like Joyce's fiction of a Jew,
the inward-looking Leopold Bloom,
likely savored a whiff of urine
on a lunch of fried kidney.

Each searched and charted the quotidien
for the briefest glimpse of the divine.
Fellow insomniacs,
in the hot-air balloon of Spinoza,
they rise through the cloudless night
taking in the vast human expanse below.
Legions of men, bird-lean or rotund,
slack abdominals on spindly legs,
reluctantly they are borne
to rarified readings and the glare
of public events.

Perhaps they are on the run
from the ultra-orthodox,
spiritual leader of the Shas,
Ovadia Yossef, a co-religionist,
though he'd deny it,
who in the Knesset one morning
rose to proclaim,
*The Reform do not belong with the people of Israel.*
*They should be vomited out!*
—the shared fate of all free thinkers.

On this side of the Atlantic,
not one to be outdone in oration,
Irish-American psychiatrist
Dr. Charles McAfferty,
Treasurer of our Analytic Society,
a gentle bull mastiff of a man
in a well-worn, three-piece Donegal tweed,
mandibles his cigar,
then rises before a boardroom filled
with the mournfully aware.
He is seasoned by nicotine, unbowed by alcohol,
as his Irish brogue thunders,
"We simply have t'do something
about this problem with the *djyoos!*"
An ashen line falls across
several wisdom-paled faces in the room.
Till it strikes him
—what his colleagues *heard*—
and he growls with amusement.
Clearing his throat,
he takes a second, more studied run:
"this problem with the *dues*".
The room deflates happily—ah, the *dues* ...

except for two analysts
who furtively check with each other,
sounding the *entendre*
to the depths.

# A Dream in Exile

At the cinema in a plush seat
I await the start of a much-hyped Coen Brothers film,
*A Serious Man*,
when someone cries for help,
pointing to a corpse wrapped in bandages
and reeking of formalin.
The body, I suspect, is that of a prophet
or forefather—Abraham?
With help, I lug him back to my seat,
now also reeking of preservative.

The film begins, but I begin
to peel away the gauze
exposing the large imploring eyes
of a darkly handsome military man,
who, in rich, clear Hebrew, proclaims, "*Hineini!*"
   (*Here I am!)*
and displays the battle injuries
he suffered in the Israeli army.

Long retired from active duty,
he was killed while strolling with his daughter
on the night before her wedding;
a sixteen-year-old, another man's daughter,
detonated a bomb belt
laced with ball bearings and nails
outside a sidewalk café in Jerusalem.

Murdered, yet summoned to my dream,
he now awaits my instruction,
and again intones, "*Hineini!*"
As if needing to pass a crucial test,
he reaches for my hand, the hand
of a man still anchored to the earth.

My film viewing sabotaged, I head home
to advise my children,
but I can no longer hear myself speak.

They look up at me in horror,
as I awaken in a cold sweat,
feeling for my face.
Am I bearded, bandaged?
Am I still here?
Why can't I just return
to being lost with the rest of the audience?

# Trans-rectal Ultrasound of the Prostate (TRUS) — with Biopsy

What a reluctant fellowship of men this is,
some older, with canes, yet several my own age, younger!
Most have heeded the pamphlet directives
and brought along a wife for support,
though there are those who, like me,
swear off all proffered comfort,
preferring to think of themselves as
lone wolves facing the lions of medicine,
and if they named this procedure "Keester Bites",
how many fewer men would volunteer to
explain a persistently elevated PSA—the spirit
of cancers yet to come?

"Steam open my letters and see if I wear a truss,"
wrote J.P. Donleavy's profligate Ginger Man,
Sebastian Dangerfield.

When I meet my radiologist, I ask,
innocent as rain: "Is there anything
the ultra-sound might show
that might make this biopsy,
er, unnecessary?"

"Ultrasounds are not specific," he replies,
handing me a consent form,
(he knows I'm a fellow medic, a psychiatrist, to boot),
then gravely confides, "There is a 1% risk
of life-threatening infection."
(Did he say "inflection"? So much
turns upon a single word.)
I sign, and prepare to undergo
the tightly scripted violation,
made gentler by the local
that burns its way around
the suspicious but unsuspecting gland.

No need to mention my gown has been lifted,
I'm high on a table, arse at the edge
as he inserts a thick plastic probe
and fine tunes it around my personal space.
"You have very tight sphincter tone,"
he notes, and how should I reply? "Sorry"
or "Thanks"? I can't decide, and choose
the silent equanimity of folded knees.

From this position I can but glimpse the radiology
screen; a smoky image (does it look like a little man?)
offers only hints as to where to find the truth.
*Now you see me, it taunts, soon you won't!*
*Location, location, location …*

"We need approximately ten tissue samples,"
he forewarns, "There will be a noise like bullets;
no need to be alarmed."
*Ka-chink! Ka-chink!*
they sound more like a staple-gun
and are far less painful than the thought of
a thick needle piercing rectum and prostate at each go.
*Ka-chink! Ka-chink!*

"You may see a little blood in your urine,
stool and sperm for two to four weeks.
This is normal." And I notice the faintest
British dispassion in his tone as I go on
counting each *Ka-chink!*
and hoping he stops at ten.

What would The Ginger Man say
about it being normal,
blood in the urine, stool and sperm?

*The pain, nay, the crime*
*of disrupting*
*normal parenchyme*

*tomato paste ejaculate*
*root beer without fizz*
*God's terrible teeth.*

Will it infiltrate my dreams,
lose me my mojo? what then?
What's a Freudian without a sex drive?
What if, not yet sixty, I'm informed,
"We found … a very small … tumor."

"The results of the biopsy will be sent
to your doctor in about two weeks," he says,
calm as an agent telling me my concert tickets
are in the mail. Then he dictates a short note
and summons a relieving stretcher.

Time is tight, too tight
to inquire about things when
the only reply is "Wait, we'll see,"
and then time becomes
a desert to cross between
question and answer.

Please check back, dear reader,
in two to four weeks; or
steam open my letters.
Me and my fellow travelers,
we have nowhere left to hide.

# Brochure

In British artist Richard Wawro's "Minnesota Farm Life",
a pasture scene fringed by amber autumn trees
is centered by cows, standing and seated, and a horse
whose neck is far too long
—all the more vital for it!
The man paints through autism, lymphoma, diabetes
—cataracts!

I lust after his dreamy "South Devon Coast, England",
with its spectral gulls reeling over maroon cliffs,
still more for his dusky "Ferry to Tiree, Scotland"
that plows the blue-green sea like a ghost-ship.
But the British pound against the Canadian loonie
makes the works as pricey as priceless,
and every one in Toronto
is packed up and shipped back to the U.K.,
unsold.

All I have left is a burning need
to read aloud what the brochure says
in biblical simplicity:
"His medium is oil crayon
and his fascination is light."

# Holy Land

# Spotting Jesus

### I.
*Outside Robinson's Supermarket, Huntsville*

Ear-ringed and bearded, he swaggers,
this mighty biker outside *Robinson's Independent,*
a huge, elaborate tattoo of a phoenix
winding 'round each of his muscular arms—
one rises from his wrist to his bicep; the other descends,
so that from its beak, emerge his fingers.
He carries a duck-headed cane—
from a motorbike accident?
Or just years of wear on these gravel roads?
The body can only take so much.
On the front of his black T-shirt
red letters scrawl a message
I would have to get too close to read,
but on the back, it declares in bold white print:
JESUS IS A CUNT.

"I trust you mean that in a not unflattering way,"
I think, beneath the brim of my Tilley hat,
my Semitic heart pulsing in its birdcage
mounted on spindly legs skirted by Bermudas.
And I wonder, having spotted Jesus
in such an unexpected place—here—
confronting this member
of Huntsville's most hardened,
which of His cheeks
would He have turned?

II.

But what of you, Lothar Stadco,
villain-faced in *The Globe & Mail* Focus piece,
"five-foot-five in motorcycle boots",
who helped The Angels set up shop in Ontario?
You, whose beefy muscles declare,
*Never testify.*
How many teens high on junk
will spot Jesus, *be* Jesus,
or rise above the need for a personal god
or the company of men
until, like a coked-up Icarus, they plummet?

Lothar, are you a warlord or domestic terrorist?
Or simply a grinning-skull patch
of protesting masculine melodrama
trying to pass for The Antichrist?

And what of the cocktail waitress
with a black satin choker,
and undercover for months,
who funneled your dealings to the cops?
Name her, Lothar,
Snitch, Ho, Rat, Bitch, posing
with uplifted bra behind her brass-topped wooden bar …

Say it somewhere in the darkness:
It is she who wears and confers
the true and fearsome mantle of grace.

# Tattoos

## I. Metro Toronto

All the porn stars have them,
so, against all I was raised to feel repelled by, in even
the word, how unattractive can they really be?

Who cares if the large one
of a butterfly at the base of the back
is dubbed a "tramp stamp" or "tramptoo",

and brings to mind
the pursuit of a French maid
by an aging lecher in a night-dress,
and not poetry?

The irreversible (or nearly so)
always means *something*, and these days,
the kids are *choosing* the ink in their skin.
Besides, tattoos accessorize well with "spacers"
that open ever-wider holes in the earlobes

which may or may not fill in
with the passing of time, or more experience:
a hope-filled young people's way of saying
they will never be sorry.

A Vietnamese girl wears
a mindful lotus
at the base of her sleek,
brown neck,

the spirited daughter of a friend
sports a tiny clump of asparagus
above her slender ankle bone, in celebration
of her lacking the gene for foul-smelling asparagus pee,

though she prefers to explain it
to curious strangers
as a tribute
to sustainable farming.

II. The Hawaiian Islands

Mike Tyson's Maori face tattoo
clearly mesmerized Oprah,
with its echoes of Polynesia and Borneo.

Native Hawaiian men sport them,
as do Hawaiian Caucasians
like the perfect blonde couple
we watch heading out on surfboards with paddles,
moving so far into the rolling ocean
you'd think they were off to fish.

The "Aloha" and "Mahalo" greetings don't impress those
who answer, "Free Hawaii!"
who resent the opulent Japanese presence,
even when multi-generational,
who resent having to work two or three jobs
just to make the rent, houses out of reach
to most of those ancestored here.

Our guide is a native Hawaiian,
with a deep baritone, a born entertainer
who finds a way to mix sex and racial politics
in a single sentence of Hawaiian history:
"My grandfather left Samoa for Hawaii to find freedom,"
he tells our tour, "which only lasted a year
—because my grandmother came right after him."

After a forceful, vocal spin through Pearl Harbor,
he regresses to an elaborate Blonde Joke,
with the punch line, *"Give her another chance!*
*Give her another chance!"*
A Blonde Joke in 2009; will we do this
for the rest of our lives?

And at the tastefully opulent Hotel Hana
we eat in the lounge rather than the dining room;
it's Hemingway-esque, and the meals are half-price
and there's live entertainment, featuring a heavy-set Hawaiian
singing love songs as he strums a ukulele.

Nowhere have I found any mark that you were here,
Matthew Makalua, though I came to look for signs of you,
one of three Hawaiian teenagers sent by King Kalakaua
to learn the secrets of Western medicine,
and save his dwindling population from leprosy,
measles, smallpox, and venereal disease
that came to Hawaii with the sailors and the priests.

You became a doctor in England, but because of your dark skin,
could not work in a hospital,
settling for a small office in your city home.

Nor could you return to the paradise of your birth,
since even a remote tie to the deposed monarchy,
overthrown with the help of the Americans,
would have landed you in jail.

That cure for leprosy the king had his eye on?
It would never have worked, if that's any comfort.

Matthew Makalua, exiled at 17,
did you sport a tattoo
against the grain
of the 19th Century you had to make do with?
If so, of what and where?
Which images of the land you came from
would have graced your arms or chest,
which letters in the language of the inker's art
been visible to all who looked you in the eye?

III. Neighborhood
*In memory of Malca Litovitz (1952 – 2005)*

On the platform of the subway
a lovely tanned woman strides by,
her shoulder-length hair swept aside

to reveal, at her nape, a heart,
and inside the heart, the word "Love"
tattooed in black and blue,

colours least likely to fade or run.
Her boyfriend must part a curtain
to admire this irrevocable gesture that

I have glimpsed in the kind of
intimate accident the body
sometimes graces us with.

And you, Malca, who left us so early
would have taken special note,
as in your poem about an orchid:

*A young girl stands in the foyer*
*waiting for a boy to notice*
*the long Wilde sleeves*
*and lace collar*
*of her Edwardian dress.*
*Her hair in a curly ponytail*
*hangs solemnly down her back.*

*New Year's Eve*
*and nothing is happening.*

# March of the Innocents

Through dark lanes they march
in silent capes of sparrows' wings: Look,

this girl and her sisters died
for her family's honor after she allowed a timid kiss,
and here is a boy who fell
to his father's drunken rages.

Here's a young girl raped and murdered
for looking pretty and helpless in pink,
and the once-proud father of a nine-year-old
"cut down outside a nightclub

he passed on his way home,
by a gun owner with a 'license to carry'
who returned, after words with a bouncer,
for a 'hail of bullets' revenge."

Prosaic, their tales of woe, and
of no consequence, to them,
the media releases that come and go.

Yet they keep marching, silent,
through dark city lanes
visible only to those who
will not forget, and those
who see the holy beings they pray to.

None of the marchers seem aware
that they are not alone,
or that, behind them,
their numbers grow.

# The Explosion at a Glock Plant in Georgia

left one man dead, though he arrived at Grady Hospital,
"in critical condition", another man in "satisfactory",
according to the spokesman; and a woman, unhurt
though dazed, like the witness to a sniper's spree
awake for everything; it is most likely she who will
develop "post-traumatic stress"
so much later than one might ever guess—

But after the explosion's hour on *Yahoo!*
all news of it vanished into the ether.
Only the *Augusta Chronicle* wrote it up,
while the *Michigan Shooter* never asked:
When an explosion takes out a gun plant,
how many lives are *saved?*
Instead, the magazine laments
the airlines' lack of armed pilots
and crows that a bill to ban assault rifles
would slowly be left to die—as it did.

What was the name of the man
who died that day, in the Glock plant?

I scour the web for more news of this explosion,
and finding none, news of explosions at other gun plants,
all 2,000 of them, the glimmering origins
of somebody's death, functioning and whole.

In other news: in California, the dough-muscled
Austro-American Action Star turned governor
campaigns *against* automatic weapons
as though he had never seen a single one of his films,
or maybe, having seen them to the point of nausea,
devoted his political life to repentance.

The Glock plant in Georgia is gone, or maybe it's
been rebuilt and joined its fellow plants
for whose music some must suffer a lacerated bowel
or undergo surgery to lift a shattered bit of skull
or spend weeks under fluorescent lights
as a trauma counselor attempts
to restore her sanity, her voice.

# FYE

In a record store called FYE
(For Your Entertainment)
a chunky, brush-cut teenager
fumbles through his wallet
at the cash counter.
I shift from foot to foot,
next in line.

As the patient, green-eyed blonde
rings through his CD purchase,
he asks her, "Do you wear a seat-belt?"
"Pardon?"
"I hope you wear a seat-belt when you drive,
'cause if I had, I might be able
to ask out someone beautiful like you."
Turning slowly, he departs,
dragging his left side.

When I step up, she runs me through,
and confides,
"He comes in here a lot,
but this is the first time
I ever heard him speak."
Her eyes moisten.
"I'm a real softy
for stories like his."

"Aren't we all?"
I mumble in cliché,
and turn away, near as slowly
to leave her graceful, efficient form
for the outside mall,
the brighter, wider world.
*Fie upon it.*

# Grandpa Martin's Dolphin

*Nassau, The Bahamas*

I'm sent by Grandpa Martin,
physicist/inventor, now legally blind,
to the Bahamian straw market
behind the Cable Beach hotel
to bargain for a sleek wooden dolphin
marked twenty-five dollars (U.S.).
"Nab it for ten, fifteen at most," he says,
"and by me, you're tops in the Kasbah."

Earlier, my wife paid twenty dollars
for four thin, gaudy beach towels.
"I couldn't help it—the woman
was limping on a huge ankle;
she had to rummage for ten minutes to find towels
in piles of shirts and sarongs.
There was a big rack of cheaper ones two stalls over,
but I spotted them too late.
Guess *I'm* no bargainer."

Now I am torn between the book I am reading
on our trip, *The Known World* by Edward P. Jones,
about slavery in the American South, while I
vacation in the slave trade's demographic wake
with guidebooks that are clear on this:
prices are inflated; the natives *expect* you to haggle.

On a tour of downtown Nassau
our driver-and-guide announced,
"Aroun' here it's thee parents, not thee kids
that is thee boss. If they draw or paint on a wall,
they out o' school, and have to learn thee trade."
And passing police headquarters,
"Most o' those men that wind up in thee jail,
that's because they hit thee wives."

When I return to the straw market,
an imposing woman wrapped in a brightly coloured,
diaphanous shawl takes me on:
"I cahn't let thees go fuh fifteen.
Dee men do da cahrvin', and we jest do da sellin'.

"We don't set dee prices."
A lie, perhaps, but everything is at work
within my mind. Can I send her home
to a black eye for nearly giving away
the fruits of her man's labour?

She wants twenty-five for the dolphin;
its light colour would be lost on grandpa's failing eyes.
It's only worth fifteen, but that will take pressure.
"Twenty."
I swallow.
Had she spotted
me scouting the market in advance
for what my father-in-law had stroked
with his bare hands?

"Twenty," she huffs,
swiftly wrapping it
in tissue and a plastic bag.

A week later,
my wife's dad considers his holiday gift:
"Out of curiosity,
how much did you end up paying?"
(Like his daughter, he's no negotiator
but he does love a well-argued price.)
"Um, not ten, I'm afraid.
Fifteen, on your behalf
and five more out of guilt
at the hours it must take
to carve such a likeness."

"Hours?
More like a couple quick coats of varnish.
Most of this stuff is machine-lathed
to a program.
Up there, in my collection, you see
that eagle I bought from a Native in Alaska?"

"The one in dark wood?"

"That's the one."

"Bring it here. Turn it over."

"Made in Mexico."

And there's the moment I ask myself:
Is this *all* we do? Just *use* each other?

# Grandpa Martin Asleep

White-haired with black eyebrows,
arms folded, stretched long on a couch,
retired from the ion spectrometer he invented
to keep airplanes free
of explosives, Martin, the physicist sleeps—

not suspecting Betsy, his wife, my wife's mother,
gingerly approaching, holding a red woolen blanket
with white fringes.

Will one of them tickle him awake?
Over his softly breathing form she finesses it,
saving for last, the spot where his trouser leg has hitched
to expose a stretch of flesh gone hairless and white.

It's a good sleep,
being meticulously
loved.

# Head Shots

The new century looms as a concrete barrier.
The severed head and slit throat have made a comeback
amid the screams of fleeing civilians
who simply want to go on living.

The burned boy seems immaterial.
Two men lug him by his hands and feet,
like a ruined rug to the dump.

Crowds march, chanting, berating,
and hoisting blow-ups of tribal celebrities.
At a party, a surgeon tells me, "We're going to fail in Iraq
because we're reluctant to torture

in order to gain the Enemy's respect;
forget what you know about winning hearts and minds."
Soon after, news breaks about Abu Ghraib,
and that night, I see my surgeon friend's head in a dream.

(He had lost his father young, too early
to dazzle him with his success.
Yet, he seemed determined to hold
his head high, no matter what the body count.)

His heart, invisible at that moment,
beat in his sacred chest. He praised
violent acts, cleansings, purgings, *débridements*,
all in "cultural self-defense".

To my friend's balding head
I blurted, *Why expect the world to see
noble motives in your incursions?
No one else can know your heart.*

But it beat, and spun the great wheel for other men,
other women, the children of others, and its beating
wished them luck, even as our metals pierced
their terrified minds and hearts.

But *here*'s a new disembodied head—
No! it's a live man, buried in clay up to his neck.
Could it be old Joe Bendit, that spinner of late-night tales,
only no longer able to declaim

on the robbers and rapists
and crooked politicians of his fabled Istanbul?
And *there*, just a few yards away, up to *his* neck in working-class irony
is *Dad,* still carrying on with choice songs

from the Thirties, Forties and Fifties.
*These golden oldies have I shored*
*against my ruin*, he might just as well say.
Only now, he borrows work from the john in the old CPR
Railway station:

*One would think/ with all this wit*
*that Shakespeare's goat/ came here to shit.*
How could new-world civilians like Joe and Dad
have ended up so deep in it,

just because some surgeon and his friends decided,
"to go over there and kick some dictator's ass?"
How far is Joe's Istanbul from Iraq,
from the flesh-pots of the Bible,

the gates of Bush and Cheney's Washington,
Putin's Mother Russia revival,
Mr. Hu's one-car-per-family fantasyland,
Ahmadinejad's nuclear Iran?

*Let them all go to hell!* cry Dad and Joe,
wiggling their ears and noses,
but their breathing grows laboured
and their heads are shot through

with worn clichés and anecdotes
like over-processed cheese,
and convictions tossed hot into the air
that neither ever dreamed he would die for.

# Razor Wire

I like to feel my late father's straight razor
dance about my neck.
His barber scissors, too, have kept their edge
and, as long as they do, I feel justified

to have two sweat-scented steel blades
join me in outlasting him.
(Hard, though, to understand the loss
incurred by those who held their fathers dear.)

True, your boy never wrote into existence
a single living human being, let alone a real dog,
or captured what it was about you, Dad,
that made you so difficult for so long.

The other day I slighted your name
before a group of dinner guests,
then grew ashamed of having slagged the dead
and for letting it be known
how unfinished we let everything get.

# fresh

*"Elle a perdu sa frâicheur."*
— *Pigault-Lebrun, French novelist*

The unassuming green-lettered sign
over the restaurant
reads "Fresh",
subtitled "Run by Juices for Life".

Inside, in subdued light,
an Annex longhouse from the Sixties
with echoes of Seattle
in the very heart of Toronto.
Down a pier of two-seater tables
sit healthy-enough types,
some with Gothic pallor
and a drug-slimmed lifestyle—
marks of the art world's asceticism
with periodic lapses of the munchies.

From a counter-cultural menu
I choose a baby jungle of greens
along with shreds of organics
topped with medallions of grilled tofu steak,
toasted sunflower seeds
and some purple kelp *en vinaigrette.*

My server, 'Tasha
is among the new bare-bellied
warriors, a young woman unafraid
to take my order
with breath faintly smelling
of red onion.

Chopsticks poised, I ignore the urge
to chat up two sinewy, tie-dyed women
an elbow's length away
as the blenders come on,
two or more at a time,
with the din of a chorus of leaf blowers
arrived to ravage a picnic,

but even in the briefest exchange
of light between us,
it dawns in their eyes and I am revealed:
*The Old Guy in the Room.*

# Massimo's

Lusting for extra-virgin olive oil
laced with balsamic drizzled
over a bed of ripe tomatoes,
I arrive in Massimo's

where men sport beer bellies, honestly come by,
proudly shirted on display.
The tables are surfaced with two shades of speckled stone.
An ancient fan whirs its welcome over the door.

Seated under the heavy, loosely (it seems) bolted TV,
a beautiful woman smiles at her boyfriend.

With a trace of an Italian accent,
I order "a Caprese"
leaving out the word "salad".

A former patient enters with her beau,
spots me, and opts for take-out. It's par
for the course in my work, a sudden
meeting with the need to not be wanted.

Here the pizza is served in long wedges,
like scrolls; I came here to belong,
and now I don't, twice over, and
I lose what I am seeing, seeing instead
the way someone else thinks I should see it,
and I think, that in this place of sketchy washrooms
down a steep flight of stairs, between close walls,
one could easily, if mistakenly, get whacked
—*Snap out of it, Ron!*

Within a few years the place will vanish in the flames
of re-location, but I remember now, that before I came here,
I read George Amabile's "Basilico",
a poem about lost love,
not suspecting it would send me on a quest
for fresh basil, extra-virgin olive oil,
balsamic vinaigrette
and this.

# Seeking Jacques in Caesarea

I keep returning to Jacques in Caesarea,
*restauranteur* and determined *bon vivant* who infused a powerful
    green tea with herbs
and left us by the edge of the sea with three kinds of
    complimentary gelati
to gaze past his canvas umbrellas at two shades of
    Mediterranean,
the harbour-side pure turquoise, the further a more exacting
    blue,
if later valium-ized by the digital developing process.

I am seeking Jacques in Caesarea, recalling how, handsome and
    sun-baked,
he challenged us to guess his age, then confessed that his
    business varied
with the time of the day, and the weekend, and the threat of war,
and that it was nearing the point of success, which he could tell
"from the shrinking size of my overdraft".

I identify a faint French lilt to his voice, loud and resonant for 76,
And his sleeves are slightly rolled above the blue tattoo numbers.
He arrived in Israel from Auschwitz, Poland via Southern France,
"from the fry-pan into the fire", and, for a short time,
Reno, Nevada, of all places, and he proudly informs us,
    "I never speak
a single word in Hebrew; why should I,
when all you ever get is an argument?"

By the broad sweep of beach where there once stood
    a Hippodrome,
I keep conjuring this proud, melancholy survivor Jacques,
not because he helped us identify as Druze
the Arabic tourists with women in black dresses
    and white headscarves,
and not because he accurately predicted
    that not a single one of them
would stop by for his frozen gelati or powerful tea,
but because he remade himself on an ideal point
near the wind-swept jetty at Caesarea,
the last stand of a man who met the Nazis up close,
and for whom a big overdraft held no terror,
yet who, nearing 80, still sought to impress on us
    his success,

in all its temperamental form,
in a man no less argumentative than any Israeli
or Israeli-Arab cabby, though one grown accustomed
    to whitecaps
dancing on the soft sweep of broken sand at Caesarea,
where Romans declared order before mapping
their gentile empire by marching across it back home.

# I'm drawn to the Feltzners

I'm drawn to the Feltzners, Dov and Daouda:
he, Israeli, she, Palestinian, father and mother
of two, and both as secular as an all-you-can-eat buffet.
If you needed the shoes off their feet, you'd have them.

When my daughter had an assignment on
        the Holocaust,
Dov raided his restaurant for two legs of lamb
that she could use in her carnage display.
And once, in an airplane, I got to sit beside Daouda
and saw firsthand how being Palestinian is
always being wary away from home.

On occasion, I question them on the prospects for peace,
perhaps just to hear someone who knew as much as they did
tie the word together with "always hope,"
though last time we talked of it, they conjured
children with the faces of ghetto survivors
on the Palestinian side of the fence.

But whatever you do, said Dov Feltzner,
do not give Hitler—or bin Laden!—a belated victory.
Then he spread his arms
and took a run straight for his statuesque wife
as if he were The Second Plane
but she could stop him—and did, embracing him,
in fact, as if by the sheer force of their personal lives,
the two of them could re-shape the world.

# A Final Hallelujah

*News item: Leonard Cohen asks that performing artists desist from recording his much-covered song "Hallelujah"*

Lord, grant us *gravitas*
if not for what we have been,
then for what we have seen:

so many sisters and brothers
swept away by
the undertow of Creation,

so many bodies
recovered
with unrecognizable
faces.

Grant us the grace
of a wise old man
who pleads no contest
to failing anatomy,

but immerses
in the inevitable sway
of the elements.

Spare us the fate of women
who become sport for armed warriors,
until murdered, at the point
past novelty.

Lord who bade Leonard Cohen
write "Hallelujah",
and delivered it
unto k.d. laing to sing,

Lord of our ancestors,
Lord of the candles,
God of Small Things,

Take full measure of our verse
even as we ready the hearse
and prepare to deliver

one more of our kind
to your calibrated
mercy.

Grant us *gravitas*
at the lowering
of the burial cables,

if not for what we have been,
for what we have seen,
and, so often,
borne alone.

## Acknowledgments

"Minimalist" was first published in *The Fiddlehead*.
"Istanbul" and "Rummy" were published in *The Windsor ReView*.
"Synagogues I Sat In", "Holocaust by Proxy" and "Tattoo"
were first published in *Parchment*.
"Massimo's" was first published in *The Medical Post*.
"An Explosion at a Glock Plant", formerly titled "Glockenspiel"
was first published in *Ars Medica*.
"Seeking Jacques in Caesarea" first appeared in *Descant*.
"Mylar" first appeared in *The Canadian Medical Association
Journal, CMAJ*.

The phrase "The Adjudicator of Pain" derives from a talk
given by professor of psychiatry Vivian Rakoff.

Editorial input was provided by Susan Ioannou,
John B. Lee and Andy Patton. Richard Harrison
undertook the final editing and helped shape the manuscript.

No character in these poems is identical to any living person.

This book is dedicated to Betsy (Elizabeth) and Martin Cohen.